SO YOU WANT TO WIN HER BACK?

Tough-Love Advice
For The Alcoholic Husband
- Or Any Other Man -
Who Wants To Save His Marriage

Also by Wren Waters:

The Alcoholic Husband Primer: Survival Tips For The Alcoholic's Wife

SO YOU WANT TO WIN HER BACK?

Tough-Love Advice
For The Alcoholic Husband
- Or Any Other Man -
Who Wants To Save His Marriage

by Wren Waters

Introduction

The purpose of my life is being a father to my kids
and being a husband to my wife.

- Terrence Howard

If you're reading this book, I am going to suggest it is for one of two reasons:

First, you're a man who recognizes he has a drinking problem (or some other kind of marital problem), fears he's losing his wife and wants desperately to save his marriage and win her back.

Wonderful!

What you read here may not be what you *want* to hear but I hope you trust it may be what you *need* to hear. Alcoholism and its effects look and feel *a whole hell of a lot different* from her side than from yours. When you read what I have to say, you may think it was not "like that" or "that bad" but trust me – it probably was. (Is?)

That's one possible reason for the why and how this book has found its way into your hands.

The second possible reason isn't so easy.

The second possible reason you're reading this book is because you're a guy who may or may not think he has a drinking problem but *your wife does!*

And she gave you this book!

If that's the case, there's a good chance you're none-too-happy about reading this book. (And if you're still actually reading this, I applaud you!) You're probably not going to be much happier about what I have to say. No one really wants relationship advice from an outsider, much less some relatively anonymous chick sitting at a typewriter. (Ok, computer key board but you get the idea.) And the idea of actually *hearing AND implementing what said chick has to say...*

Well, that's entirely up to you but before you toss me (aka this book) in the fire, may I offer you at least one bit of advice:

If your wife gave you this book, I am going to wager it's her last-ditch effort to save your marriage. I'm going to go out on a limb and say she has been mentally packing her bags *for years* and is now close to literally packing her bags. I am even going to be so ballsy as to say if your wife has given you this book, more of her wants to leave than wants to stay.

She is desperate.

She is scared.

She is tired.

She is overwhelmed.

And she is pretty much DONE!

But there's a little piece of her still wanting.

Still wishing.

Still hoping.

And so she has given you this book in an effort to try *one more thing* before she gives up completely on you and the marriage.

I know because I am that woman.

The only difference between your wife and me is that while your wife read the book (at least enough to know she wanted you to read it) I wrote the book.

Why did I write this book?

Because my husband is an alcoholic.

When you are married to an alcoholic, you think about it *all the time*. You don't want to. You simply can't help yourself.

One day I was contemplating whether or not it was "too late" for my husband to win me back – if he ever felt like he wanted to that is. My husband and I are not divorced physically but we are divorced emotionally. We are two people living separately together under one roof.

"What would I need from my husband," I asked myself.

What would he have to do to repair our marriage from the ravages of his compulsive drinking? Could he even fix this marriage that is barely even a marriage now?

What follows are the my answers to my own questions.

I don't know that this will be an "easy" read for you, the husband. Quick, yes. Easy? I don't know. And you may want to dismiss things I say because this is my life, my answers, my experience. Fair enough *except* I will tell you this one universal truth about the alcoholic marriage::

Every alcoholic marriage is the same – just in different ways.

The particulars maybe different but the emotions are the same. Every woman married to an alcoholic feels the same anger, resentment, despondency, heartsickness, wrath, bitterness, hopelessness…

And hopefulness.

Your wife doesn't necessarily *want* to leave you but she has come – or is quickly coming – to the point where she *needs* to leave you.

Whoever you are and whatever brings you to be reading this

book, I want to acknowledge your bravery. It's not easy looking at our own flaws or shortcomings and it's even less easy having them pointed out to us by a stranger hiding behind the pages of a book. But sometimes, if our lives aren't working, if our relationships are suffering, maybe that's exactly what we need.

I'm not an "expert" or a therapist. I am a woman living the same or a very similar life to the life your wife feels she is living. I am a woman who may be saying *the same damn things* your wife has been saying (harping on) for years.

(Or I may be saying things that you had *no idea* your wife was feeling or experiencing.)

Either way, this is not about attacking you.

It's not about making you feel like a dick.

It's not about throwing everything and the kitchen sink at you in terms of why your marriage is failing.

It's about (hopefully) giving you a woman's perspective – dare I say your wife's perspective - on what has happened to her and your marriage since alcohol became a third partner.

When it's gone, you'll know what a gift love was.
You'll suffer like this.
So go back and fight to keep it.

- Ian McEwan, "Enduring Love"

SUGGESTION #1

WHY DO YOU HAVE TO DO ALL THE WORK?

So here you are, reading a book about how to win back your wife. Maybe you picked it up yourself, maybe your wife shoved it in your face but either way, your marriage is in trouble and this book is in your hands.

It's not you don't love your wife.

You do.

That's why (by coercion or choice) you're reading this book.

And you or her or both of you say alcohol is the issue.

But now you (YOU!) seem to have to do everything (EVERYTHING!) to win her back and save the marriage.

Yep. That's pretty much it.

If you can concede and accept the premise that it's all on you for the time being, go ahead and skip ahead to Suggestion #2.

But if any part of you (or all of you) is bristling at the idea that you have to do all the work, all the changing, all the fixing, stay right here and I'll (try to) explain.

Compulsive drinking (i.e. alcoholism) erodes *everything.*

And I mean everything.

Trust, intimacy, joy.

It's nuclear run-off in the ground water of your life and your wife's life.

It has been affecting – for a long time I assure you - how your wife feels about you, about herself, about her life, about her children, about her parenting, about her house.

ABOUT EVERYTHING!

One more time, just for emphasis:

A husband's alcoholism affects EVERYTHING about his wife's life.

And so when you realize you don't want to lose her, the onus is on you because – at the risk of sounding like a second grader – you started it.

Do you have a right to have your feelings heard and validated?

Is it reasonable that you have an expectation that you wife put forth her own efforts to heal the marriage? Should she be required to contribute mentally, emotionally, spiritually and physically to the repair of the relationship?

Yes.

Of course.

Eventually.

But not at first.

At this point, for now, it's all on you.

Let me tell you something:

Your wife is *one pissed off chick!*

She is *mad!*

And she is *resentful!*

She remembers shit from your drinking episodes that you would *swear* never happened! It's not she's storing these things up. She doesn't even necessary *want* to remember. But sometimes things happen that refuse to be forgotten.

She has spent a long time now hating you.

And loving you.

Giving up on you.

And hoping for you.

She's cried for you and over you more than you know.

She's cried while doing laundry, walking the dog, and sitting in her car in the driveway, too afraid to drive away, too afraid to come back in.

She's cried in the bathroom and at work and in the middle of the night while you (blissfully?) slept off another bender.

She has cursed your name, dammed your soul and then shook it all off so she could cook dinner for you and your kids like a 21st century Donna Reed. (Google her if you're under 40….)

And yet she's still here.

Why?

Because she loves you.

Because she doesn't want to give up on you.

Because her marriage and her vows matter to her.

Believe it or not, most women don't want to end their marriages, even when their husband has a serious drinking issue. Most women try as long as they can to hold onto their marriages. In a society where it seems no one takes their marital vows seriously, there are women who do.

And you are married to one of them.

But women are emotionally complicated.

Things get into us, become part of our beings and we can't simply shed them like a snake shedding her old skin. We can't just "forget" because one day you're ready to.

I know it's different for men.

I know most men would prefer to handle a difficult past by simply putting it in the past and moving forward.

But it's not so easy for women.

We don't really do well with our husbands simply waking up one day and saying,

"Hey honey, what do ya say we have a 'do over' of our marriage? You know, like the last ten or 15 or 20 years when I've been drunk and calling you names and pretty much treating you like shit? What do ya say we just forget about that and start anew from here. Sound good to you?"

Your drinking started it all and so - for awhile anyway - it's going to have to be you who does it all when it comes to regaining her trust, re-igniting her love and winning her back.

There is nothing inherently interesting about being a drunk
– in fact quite the contrary.

- Heather King, "Parched: A Memoir"

I had made her so unhappy that she developed a sense of humor.

- Kurt Vonnegut, Bluebeard

SUGGESTION #2

ACKNOWLEDGE WHAT YOUR DRINKING
HAS DONE TO HER

My husband has called me a fucking bitch…

Told me to fucking shut up…

And wished upon me to fucking die.

He's told me everything is all my fucking fault, that I am fucking psycho and that he hopes one day I walk in front of a fucking bus.

He's screamed (SCREAMED!) at me for eating a piece of bacon, thrown my shoes out of the bathroom in a tirade because he "HATES FUCKING SHOES IN THE BATHROOM" and one time told me to go ahead and "fucking walk," when we got into an argument in the car. He even pulled over so I could get out.

I was pregnant.

And I've heard worse (a lot worse even!) from other wives.

If I reminded him of any of these things, and others, he would swear (SWEAR) with his last dying breath that he indeed, did NOT do or say such things. Not that much. Not as often as I remember or "as bad" as I remember.

And you know, I'd kind of believe he would believe himself. I have no doubt he is deeply ashamed and aghast at things he has said to me while under the influence. He needs to deny. For himself.

So I am not here to remind you of all the possibly horrible, despicable, humiliating thing you did when you were drunk or drinking.

I'm just saying don't deny it didn't happen the way your wife remembers.

I can guarantee (G-U-A-R-A-N-T-E-E) you that your drinking did not FEEL to your wife the same way it FELT to you. Drunk people – whether the occasionally drunk or chronically drunk – are never as funny, witty, sensitive, engaging and/or as magnanimous as they think they are.

And they are always (ALWAYS) meaner, crueler, more hostile, obnoxious, brutal and viscous than they realize or remember.

Being married to an alcoholic is like standing outside your house…

And watching while someone (you love!) inside takes a sledge hammer to every single thing in the house. Furniture, walls, knickknacks. Pets. CHILDREN! Even your future. Yes, being married to an alcoholic feels like someone is sledgehammering *your future.*

And if you want to win your wife back, you have to acknowledge that. That's not to say you have to drag your soul through every horrible detail of the past years. Now is the time for moving forward and you're allowed to put the past in the past.

But don't tell you wife or try to convince her that it wasn't *as bad* as she remembers.

Forgive someone today. Especially if that someone is you.

- Gina Greenland,
"Postcards and Pearls: Life Lessons from
Solo Moments On The Road"

SUGGESTION #3

FORGIVE YOURSELF

Yeah, one for you!

Actually it's not.

This is for her too.

Yes, forgiving yourself is for her but hey, you reap some pretty good benefits as well.

Why do I say forgive yourself?

And why do I say it's for her, not you?

Maybe you've already realized this but in case you haven't, allow me please to point a little something out:

Alcoholics have, shall we say, the *tendency* of projecting a lot (all?) of their self-hatred and loathing onto those around them. And when it comes to the alcoholic husband and his wife, it's projection on steroids. I didn't always know this or understand the dynamic but after years of living with, reading about, talking about, thinking about and trying to figure out my alcoholic husband, it was one fight - with one simple but profound statement from him - that pulled back the-wizard's-behind-the-curtain-curtain for me.

I can't even remember what the fight was about but, as typical in the alcoholic marriage, the yelling and screaming was far disproportionate to whatever the issue was.

Finally my husband screamed at me,

"JUST LOOK AT YOURSELF!"

I had no idea what he was talking about and demanded he explain himself.

He refused. Or that's what I thought initially.

His "accusation" did end the fighting and the screaming and we retreated to our own physical and mental spaces.

And that's when it hit me.

It's not he *wouldn't* explain himself.

He *couldn't*.

And the reason he couldn't is because what he really meant was, "Just look at me."

What he was really saying was,

"Just look at me. Look at what I am becoming. Look at what I am doing. Look at who I fear I am."

You do terrible, horrible things when you are an alcoholic.

You do things that are too humiliating to remember.

You treat the people you love the most the worse. Worse than you would treat a friend, a co-worker, an acquaintance…a stranger on the street!

And then you blame everyone around you because the burden, the shame, the knowledge is just too heavy a burden to bear.

Put it down.

Forgive yourself.

I mean it.

Completely, 100%, without reservation

As the wife of a man who has said horrible, horrible things to me – often in front of our children – I will tell you, if you forgive yourself, she will forgive you too.

But you can't forgive yourself with excuses, justifications or an asterisk, so to speak.

You can't say,

"I forgive myself but…

"If she hadn't…"

"She did too…"

"It's not like I…"

You have to simply forgive yourself.

Look yourself in the eye and say,

"Ok, you were certainly a prick…

And I forgive you.

It's not going to be easy because you never wanted to hurt your wife the way you did.

You never wanted to treat her the way you did.

You never wanted to be or do any of the things alcohol made you be or do.

Not a single wife of an alcoholic (and I've talked to LOTS of them) has ever said,

"My husband was an ass-hole before the alcohol."

Nope, not a one.

Every single wife I've spoken with has always said,

"This was not the man I fell in love with."

Your wife remembers the man you were.

Before the drinking.

She wants and grieves and wishes for the man you were.

Before the drinking.

Forgive that man.

Your wife knew him to be kind, fun, loving, compassionate, committed, loyal.

Forgive that man and kick the alcoholic impostor to the curb.

I felt ashamed for what I had done. I don't have any excuses.
I did what I did. I take full responsibility for myself and my actions.
I wouldn't pawn this off on anybody. I'm sorry it happened.
I hurt people.

- Louie Anderson

My wife heard me say I love you a thousand times,
but she never once heard me say sorry.

- Bruce Willis

SUGGESTION #4

APOLOGIZE TO YOUR WIFE

Ok, this might be (one of) the hard parts.

No one really likes to apologize and with all due respect, I find most alcoholic husbands would rather cut off their left one than apologize.

Well, either get a knife…

Or apologize.

Because there is no way you are going to win your wife back without apologizing.

That's the bad news but I do have some good news.

It's not the long, groveling, extracted apology you might think it needs to be.

I watched a Piers Morgan interview with David Cassidy - former teen-heart throb, current alcoholic/recovering alcoholic. It was in hearing Cassidy's "apology" that I realized a) alcoholics tend to be very bad at apologizing and b) *how* the alcoholic apologizes is really, really important to the healing process for whomever he is apologizing to. If you want to hear the *wrong* way for an alcoholic to apologize, look up David Cassidy's interview with Piers Morgan.

If you want an idea on the *right* way, may I offer some suggestions?

I asked myself, what would I want to hear from my husband? What would be the "perfect" apology should he decide to apologize for the years of his alcoholic drinking and behavior? It would be something like this:

"I am sorry beyond what words can say. I can't know the full extent of how I hurt you but I know I have hurt you deeply. There is of course no way to undo or take back the way I treated you in the past but I can change the way I treat you in the future and that starts now. I'm sorry. I love you."

That's pretty much it.

You don't have to beg or grovel.

You don't have to relive every painful, ugly, regretful moment.

You just have to apologize.

Much in the same way you have to forgive yourself – sincere, fully but short and to the point – is the same way you need to apologize.

One time.

Then walk the walk.

When we love, we always strive to become better than we are. When we strive to become better than we are, everything around us becomes better too.

- Paulo Coelho, The Alchemist

SUGGESTION #5

WALKING THE WALK

Ok, so you have forgiven yourself. (You should probably re-new your self-forgiveness on a daily basis.)

And you've apologized to your wife. (One and done.)

Now here's where the rubber meets the road as they say.

You need to check back into the marriage.

As I said, every alcoholic marriage is the same – just in a different way – so maybe you weren't checked out of your marriage in the same way my husband is but you were still checked. Even if you don't think you were, you were. If you don't believe me, ask your wife.

Alcohol is a selfish, demanding bitch of a mistress.

When she was in your bed, there was no room for your wife emotionally or spiritually.

Oh you may have still rolled over and asked for or initiated sex.

You may have still had a few dates nights with your wife or gone to the obligatory PTA meeting but you weren't there much beyond your physical presence.

Mentally, emotionally, spiritually you were with Her.

Beer.

Vodka

Wine.

Rum, tequila , "Jane" Daniels."

Whatever name she went by in your life, you were with Her.

And where was your wife while you were with your mistress?

She was just trying to hold onto herself in the midst of the continual storm the alcoholic marriage is.

So your job now is to check back into the marriage and start *noticing* the woman and person you wife is.

Don't think I am asking you to grovel.

And for God's sake, please don't follow her around like a whipped puppy.

Don't feign or force 100% interest 100% of the time.

If there is anything worse than living with an alcoholic husband, it might just be living with a recovering alcoholic who is suddenly panting at your feet! Don't jump at her every need. Don't anticipate her every desire. Don't try to make up in a month what was caused over years.

Just.

Check.

Back.

In.

Just start noticing your wife again.

Noticing who she is.

If she works, ask her about work.

If she has a hobby, ask her about her latest project.

If she goes to a movie or meets a friend for dinner, when she returns home, ask her how it.

And then listen!

You may say, "Oh I never stopped doing these things" and while you may not have stopped *doing them*, I will venture you stopped actually being engaged in them.

You don't have to do a lot all at once.

For now, just work on noticing how much you stopped noticing.

'What makes the dessert beautiful,' said the little prince,
'is that somewhere it hides a well...'"

- Antoine de-Saint-Exupery, The Little Prince

The most beautiful things in the world cannot be seen or
touched, they are felt with the heart.

- Antoine de-Saint Exupery, The Little Prince

SUGGESTION #6

SEX!

Ok, who doesn't want sex in their marriage?

Well, I'll tell you.

The woman who is married to an alcoholic.

Look, I'm not trying to make you feel worse than you may already feel, but sex with an alcoholic is *the worse!*

UGG!

YUK!

"Oh God, I hope he passes out tonight so we don't have to 'do it'" kind of worse.

But wait, you wail!

"If sex with me was so bad, why did she keep having sex with me?"

Well, there are a few reasons.

First, it wasn't always bad.

Sometimes it was still good.

Sometimes you seemed to be present emotionally as well as physically.

Sometimes there was still a connection between you and her.

Sometimes she was just plain old horny herself.

Second, and if it's any constellation, this goes for wives everywhere and not just those married to alcoholics, sometimes it was just easier to say yes and get it over with then to be hounded by you all night long. I'm sure you understand. It's kind of like the same reasoning behind why you finally finish that home-improvement project.

And finally, perhaps most important of all, the reason we still have sex with our alcoholic husbands, even though we are full of anger, resentment and an ever-growing bitterness, is because we don't want to lose that one, maybe last, connection and sense of normalcy in the marriage.

I can't say it often enough.

Your wife never wanted to lose you to the drinking!

Your wife wants you back!

Your wife tried for as long as she could.

But as I said, alcohol is one nasty bitch mistress and eventually She will win if you don't kick her out of bed.

So how do you get sex NOW?

How do you get your wife to WANT to be with you once again?

Well, you're going to have to be patient.

And rebuild some trust.

And the way you do that...

Drum roll please.

Is exactly the way most men don't want to.

Physical contact and affection *without the expectation of sex.*

I know.

It's the worse!

You've actually heard this myth before but was hoping it was just that – a myth.

Nope, it's true.

Give your wife random hugs during the day, a spontaneous peck on the cheek or pat on the "cheek." Yeah, we like that when it is a playful sign of affection; not a lecherous cop of a feel.

Roll over and hold her at night *without expecting sex.*

Oh God, not that. Anything but that you say.

I'm sorry but it's true.

Here's the thing with sex and the alcoholic and the general nature of human beings.

We are sexual beings.

We are physical beings.

We like (love) physical contact between us and the person we love.

But we want the physical contact varied and to various degrees at various times.

We don't want just all humping, thumping, bumping, thrashing under the sheets.

We want the kiss that is just a kiss – not a "hey can we do it now."

We want the hug that is just a hug – not a "hey can we do it now."

We want the squeeze, the pat, the tickle that is just – you got it now - a squeeze, a pat or a tickle and not a "hey can we do it now."

The physical connection in an alcoholic marriage often becomes nothing more than the "hey can we do it now" as true intimacy deteriorates.

Your job now is to (re)create a true physical intimacy between you and your wife in place of the humping, thumping, bumping intimacy that has taken over.

And you have to be *sincere!*

When you hold her because you just want to hold her…when you hug her just to hug her…when you grab her just to be playful and affectionate, you have to REALLY be holding her just to hold her, hugging her just to be hugging her and grabbing her just to be grabbing her and not as a clandestine move to get to the humping, thumping, bumping part.

Let me tell you (assure you!) a woman can detect the true motives behind her husband's physical affection quicker and with more accuracy than an animal detecting fear.

She...

Will...

KNOW if you are just doing this out of a begrudging nod to my advice and with the real motive of having sex soon(er).

As an alcoholic, you were gone a long time.

Emotionally.

Mentally.

Spiritually.

And physically.

If you want to win your wife back, it's about returning slowly, gradually but with daily consistency and regularity.

Hug your wife.

Kiss your wife.

Give her a little squeeze.

Without any expectations but with the full knowledge that those sincere, seemingly small actions will go further in restoring your sex life than anything else you could possibly do.

Oh yeah, and one more thing.

The minute your wife starts initiating little gestures of affection again, don't take it as the green light to hop her bones. There is a lot of trust to rebuild here, including a trust that every move she makes isn't going to be interpreted as a call for sex. Believe me, when she wants to initiate sex with you, she will.

And you'll know it.

Your task is not to seek for love, but merely to seek and find all the barriers within yourself that you have built against it.

- Rumi

SUGGESTION #7

FOREPLAY BEGINS IN THE KITCHEN
(And/Or The Bathroom. And/Or
The Laundry Room. And/Or At The Florists)

So I'm sure you get my message about sex and putting yourself back in your marriage emotionally and spiritually before you push to be back (in) sexually. (No pun not intended.) Well last night something happened with my own husband and it made me think maybe I wanted to add a little more to the how-to-revive-your-sex-life-suggestion.

I think I have mentioned – maybe once or a hundred times – that my own alcoholic husband is quite checked out of our marriage. He goes to work, comes home, watches some tv, plays some video games, eats some food, goes to bed and then gets up and does the exact same thing the next day. The only difference between weekends and week days is the going-to-work part. There are nights when literally not a single word is exchanged between us.

Last night was no exception and he went to bed without me realizing it. I then inadvertently walked into our bedroom and threw on the overhead light, both blinding him and jolting him awake.

"JESUS CHRIST!" He cursed. Somewhat justifiably I will concede.

I said, "Oh, I didn't know you had gone to bed." I wanted to add, "maybe if you said good-night to your wife…" but I didn't. I just left. (Yes, I turned out the light.)

That night I fell asleep watching tv myself and didn't make it into the bedroom til around 3 am. I got into bed, curled myself up on my side as usual and started to drift off to sleep. Not five minutes later (i.e. he knew I wasn't asleep) my husband surprisingly showed what I will call some "marital interest."

I pretended to be asleep.

But what I really wanted to do was roll over and say, "you know, you'd be surprised how much simply saying good night would get ya!"

Look guys, we're emotional whores when it comes to how little you need to give in order for us to give back full-fold. That's not a bad thing. It's just how women are. We don't require or demand quid-pro-quo. But we do want some quid. And maybe a little pro now and then.

I'm telling you, if you cleaned the kitchen occasionally...

Or carried the laundry downstairs once or twice...

Or even cleaned the toilet bowel every third full moon.

You'd be amazed the return on your investment!

The best day trader couldn't get you the same "return."

Send us flowers?

Holy sex-tastic! If I may be blunt, that's like us warming you up with a blow job!

Really!

And I know there are some women who don't care for flowers. Find the equivalent! She has one, I guarantee you! The whole point is show your wife you see her, recognize her, love her, appreciate her for who she is *in addition* to the sexual being she is. Hey, we *want* to be red-hot sexy to you too! But we also want to know that our place in your life and your heart is about more than just meeting you under the sheets. And yes, as odd and counter-intuitive as it may sound, when you carry the laundry downstairs or do the dishes or clean a toilet bowel or make any sort of gesture that tells us we're more than *just* a sexual being to you, it makes us feel *more* sexual. It even makes us *want* to be more sexual. (Hey, I didn't wire women. I just explain us.)

Do not dwell in the past,
do not dream of the future,
concentrate the mind on the present moment.

- Buddha

SUGGESTION #8

STOP (OR DON'T START) TRYING TO BALANCE YOUR ALCOHOLIC BEHAVIOR

One of the red flags for me in David Cassidy's interview was when, at Pierce's prompting, David "spoke" to his wife. He apologized. Sort of. And he said, to paraphrase, he hoped she'd remember all the things he did for her, their family, *her family…*

UGG!! I wanted to scream!

I probably did.

Look, like me tell you right here and now, straight up, there is nothing…

Nothing, nothing, nothing…

Like Nothing with a capital N…

Capital O-T-H-I-N-G.

NOTH!!

ING!!

That you did in the past that will balance your alcoholic behavior.

I'm sorry but it's true.

There is not enough of anything in the world to balance out the deep, searing pain an alcoholic husband causes his wife.

There are not enough past gifts, past trips, past gestures.

I don't care if you brought her flowers everyday, ran her bath every night and took her dancing every Friday. (Which you most likely didn't. Being involved with that bitch of a mistress, Alcohol.)

I don't care if you sent her parents on annual vacations abroad, paid for her triple-nephews' braces or set her twice-divorced, three-times-removed cousin up in a Beverly Hills "cottage."

I don't care what you did – how long you did it, how often you did it or how much money it cost – because there is nothing (you know, Nothing with a capital N and all) that will balance or offset you calling her a fucking bitch or fucking whore or fucking whore and fucking bitch. Nothing to balance you telling her to shut the fuck up, go fucking die, or that she fucking disgusts you. Nothing to level out years of your drunken tirades on the holidays, humiliating spectacles in front of the neighbors or vacant nights passed out in the basement/garage/family room.

A bell can't be un-rung and alcoholic behavior can't be balanced.

My husband is generous beyond what any wife could ask when it comes to certain things in our lives. He gave freely of himself emotionally, physically and financially whenever my ailing parents needed it. He took off work when my dad had doctors' appointments, he canceled engagements when my mother needed me. He goes to work every single day and never spends the mortgage money on booze or the grocery money at a bar. He is home every single night and never questions when I go out for moms' night, go away for scrap booking weekends or take a week long art seminar three states away.

He is and has been a dream husband in many ways.

Except he is an alcoholic.

And here's the thing about alcoholics: All those wonderful things they do..

All the ways they are wonderful beings…

It doesn't make up for the drinking and it doesn't make up for the behavior.

In fact, *it makes the drinking and accompanying behavior WORSE!!!*

Yes, when you're an alcoholic and you're also an intrinsically good person who will do nice things, it makes the drinking issues hurt MORE, not LESS!

Go figure.

Because when you do those things, we see the man we know is in there.

We see the man we fell in love with.

We see the man you could be.

The man you once were.

We see the man we fear we are losing.

Apologize to your wife.

Forgive yourself.

Let it all go.

But don't try to balance or mitigate the past.

Too often we underestimate the power of a touch, a smile, a kind word, a listening ear, an honest compliment, or the smallest act of caring, all of which have the potential to turn a life around.

- Leo Buscaglia

SUGGESTION #9

MORE WALKING THE WALK

Ok, ok, ok, you say.

I get it.

Kind of

Now tell me what I need to actually *DO* to win my wife back.

Men are doers, I know that.

You don't want all this mental, emotional, feeling, thinking, examining stuff.

You want some good old ACTIONS you can take.

Right now.

Well, I don't really have anything specific for you.

Not as in a list like:

Buy her flowers every Thursday.

Take her to dinner every Friday.

Take out the trash every Saturday.

It's not that simple or easy.

(But then it is kind of simple, though probably not easy.)

Basically what you need to do is court your wife again.

Here's the thing:

I am not telling you to hang you head in shame, beg her to come back to you and spend the rest of forever jumping through every hoop imaginable (flowers, jewelry, back rubs, constant apologies, etc.) in order to win her back. And let me tell you, if your wife WANTS that, well frankly you should let her go.

I'm saying kind of the opposite.

I'm saying forgive yourself.

Hold your head up high.

And get back to being the man you were – you still are since you've read this far – and remind her why she fell in love with you in the first place.

What did you do before the A-Bitch took over?

Did you cook together?

Well when she is making the same meal for the kids the 104,345th time, go ahead and help her. You don't need to recreate your romantic Friday night cooking with a glass of wine in hand. (You can't recreate that anyway. You know the whole alcoholic thing plus there are kids now plus five or ten or 20 years have passed since those nights.) It's not the particulars you need to recreate anyway.

It's the sentiments.

The emotions.

It's **THE CONNECTION!** *(*As in between you and her.)

She has felt alienated and abandoned by you for a long, long time now. She's weary, hesitant, uncertain about you. About the marriage. About the two of you.

You can't come rushing in all flower-giving-guns a blazing and expect her to jump back into your arms.

So if you want to know what *To Do* exactly , ask yourself these questions: (there I go again, more of this thinking, feeling, examining stuff . Sorry…)

What was it about her that made you fall in love with her in the first place?

What was it about you that made her fall in love with you?

What did you enjoy doing for her *before* (the alcoholic Bitch mistress took over)?

What did the two of you enjoy doing together?

What do you think she needs, wants, craves from you now?

There are certain things you could do *now* that are like total freebies as in all you have to do is pay attention and DO THEM and you'dget like mega-bonus points. What are those things? Well, I don't know what they would be specifically for you and your wife but I'll share a few from the list I would make for my husband should he ever ask. In no particular order:

Put the *&$#(@ flippin' toilet paper ON! THE! HOLDER!!

AND THROW AWAY THE EMPTY CARDBOARD ROLL!!

Close the kitchen cabinet doors!!!

Don't leave trash on the kitchen counter.

Pick up his socks.

Carry the laundry downstairs without me asking.

Clean the kitchen the nights I work.

I hope you get the idea and I'll let you in on a little secret:

All these things are normal things that normal wives in normal (i.e.non- alcoholic) marriages complain about. The problem is in the alcoholic marriage, these annoying but mundane infractions take on a bigger significance in your wife's mind. I know they did for me.

My thought pattern went something like this:

"I have to put up with him calling me a fucking bitch and he can't even close the &*$@ kitchen cabinet doors?!"

That's the bad news.

The (ironic) good news is because of the alcoholic history of your marriage, you will actually get MORE credit for stepping up and addressing these things than your plain old, typical slaker-but-not-alcoholic-husband counterpart!

Be happy for this moment. This moment is your life.

- Omar Khayyam

SUGGESTION #10

NO KEEPING SCORE

Ok, let's be honest.

Human beings are selfish creatures.

Some are selfish in that they'd-take-your-arm-off-for-the-last-marshmallow-encrusted-sweet-potato-at-Thanksgiving sort of way while others are simply selfish in that human-condition sort of way.

No one does anything for "nothing."

Even the apparently most selfless person does what he or she does for a need it fulfills in them.

And so, all the feel good wedding vows and marriage advice not withstanding, even the healthiest, happiest, most giving couples give to each other with an expectation of *something* in return.

And so when you come out of your shell, when you check back into your marriage, when you realign yourself with your wife's needs and desires, eventually your thoughts are going to wind themselves around to something like,

"Hey! When do I start getting something in return?"

Well, I'm not going to say you don't have the right – or at the very least the innate nature – to feel this way.

I'm just saying you can't really indulge those feelings quite yet.

Here's the problem:

Have you seen that commercial for FitBit where the guy leaves his house and starts running, running, running. Oh he is running. He is pushing himself beyond his limit. He is doing this! RUN-NING!

SO!

FAR!

And then he looks at his FitBit and it says "three tenths of a mile!"

And his wife pops her head out their upstairs window and yells "you're doing great honey."

He was sure he had run miles and miles when in reality…

He hadn't even run far enough to be out of range of his bedroom window!

When you haven't really been, uh, shall I say that "giving" in your relationship and then you decide your going to start giving…

It can feel kind a like that.

Like you have been giving and giving AND GIVING when in reality it's only been about "three tenths of a mile" worth of giving.

I know what you (may be) thinking.

What the hell?

"You're saying I just have to give and give and give to my wife and my wife gets to just sits back and take and take and take? You sound just like my wife!"

Yeah, funny how that works.

But no, I am not saying you have to give and give and give and never receive.

I'm saying your wife feels like she has been giving and giving and giving and giving AND GIVING for a long, long, LONG time now without you giving back. And so when you start giving back to the marriage, a) it's going to feel like a lot more to you than it does to her. Initially anyway and b) you've got a few (ok, many) layers of pissed-off-wife to get through before she's ready to check back in herself. If you're spending everyday putting tally marks on a mental or emotional scorecard, you're going to get angry and feel defeated and give up.

And hey, that's not what you've come here for.

That's not why you have hung in here and read this &%$#* book this far!!

I guarantee you, if you stay the course, your wife will come back.

You just have to be willing to let her do it on her time frame, not yours.

When a woman is talking to you,
listen to what she says with her eyes.

- Victor Hugo

Women speak two languages – one of them is verbal.

- William Shakespeare

SUGGESTION #11

HEAR HER OUT

You want to know something really (really!) annoying about women?

We need to talk things out.

Oh, you already knew that?

Ok, well did you know that talking things out really does make them go away for us?

Which is a particularly cruel trick our creator played on us because the way most men need, want or prefer to make things go away is by pretending they have gone away. If a tree falls in the forest, sort of thing. If you never talk about an issue with your wife, is there really an issue? Well, guess what? For your wife, the *more* you *don't* talk about an issue, the more of an issue it becomes.

Do you know WHY the time you did X or Y or XY keeps coming up again and again and again even though it's been YEARS?! Because your wife didn't get to completely process it. She didn't get to mash it around like a cow chewing its cud. She didn't get to totally eviscerate it from her mind and heart. So it's in there still. Maybe just a tiny piece of it. Maybe 99% of it is over for her but that 1% is still gnawing and nagging at her. That 1% wants and needs its due.

I know, I know.

"Come on!" You want to say.

"I can't talk about that shit for one minute more!!"

I get it. I do.

But may I offer one bit of insight as to why you feel like you are talking about the same "shit" over and over and OVER again:

Because you didn't do it "right," i.e. talk about it the way you wife needed - the first time.

It's like me and painting. I hate painting. I hate preparing the surface even more. And so I do a half-assed prep job and then have to listen a year later as my husband tells me (again!) why it is I need to repaint.

Look, I know you'd rather stab daggers into your eyes. Or pull your own fingernails out. Or listen to 100 long-tailed cats in a room full of rocking chairs than talk about an "issue" once, much less more than once . And I know there is a real emotional pain to discussing, ad nausea, things you wife feels you did "wrong." It makes men very, very uncomfortable to have their every word and action dissected to the nth degree. And when the incidents or infractions were months or even years ago? And when it includes being reminded of drunken behavior from years gone by?

Where's that room full of cats?

Unfortunately you kind of have to go through this. If it's any consolation, it's more *for her* than *about you*. She doesn't want you to fix or undo anything- or feel like a big giant jerk all over again. What she wants, needs is to know that you are really hearing and understanding what her feelings are or were regarding the issue (s). And until she feels like you have really (really!) heard her, the things she is holding onto will not go away. They will be like little tiny pieces of splinter in her heart – festering and growing in an intensity that threatens to become even bigger than whatever the original issue may have been.

Alcohol ruined me financially, morally, broke my heart and the hearts of too many others. Even though it did this to me and it almost killed me and I haven't touched a drop in 17 years, sometimes I wonder if I could get away with drinking some now. I totally subscribe to the notion that alcoholism is a mental illness because thinking like that is clearly insane.

- Craig Ferguson,
America On Purpose: The Improbable
Adventures of an Unlikely Patriot

Tell your heart the fear of suffering
is worse than the suffering itself.

- Paulo Coelho, The Alchemist

SUGGESTION #12

STOP DRINKING

Ha, so you thought you were going to get by without this one.

I will admit I initially had this as suggestion Number One!

I mean it is kind of obvious that if you have a drinking problem – or you wife believes you do anyway – and said drinking problem is the original source – again, at least per your wife – of your marital issues, then in order to fix those issues and win her back, you are going to have to…

Drum roll please.

Yes, I'm going to say it.

Stop.

Drinking.

Yes, of course you already knew this.

That's why I buried it back here.

And because I wanted you to realize there is far more to saving your marriage than *just not drinking anymore.*

There tends to be a fair amount of frustration among some recovering alcoholics who quit drinking but find their marriages don't spontaneously heal. They are confused, hurt, angered even that they did *the one thing* their wife has been nagging, begging, demanding of them and yet she *still* isn't happy!

Yes, you have to quit drinking.

But I hope the first nine suggestions have helped you to see that there is far more work to be done than simply not drinking.

Not that there is anything simple about not drinking for the alcoholic.

Your struggle with alcohol is real and tenacious, convoluted and complicated. It hasn't been easy and it's probably been a long time coming for you to arrive at this point where you can acknowledge and accept that your alcohol consumption is pretty much responsible for *all* the problems between you and your wife.

But what if you don't agree with your wife and her assertation that you have an issue with alcoholic?

In fact, what if you *know* you don't have a drinking problem?!

Ok, well maybe you do, maybe you don't.

(You probably do.)

At this point, it actually doesn't really matter if you do, you don't or you think you don't.

The point is *your wife thinks you do!*

And because your wife thinks you do and because you want to save your marriage and win her back, you need to stop drinking.

"What?!" You want to scream.

"Just because my wife thinks I have a drinking problem, I'm the one who has to stop drinking?!"

No, you don't have to stop drinking "just" because your wife thinks you have a drinking problem. You have to stop drinking because you *know* you have marital problems and for your wife the heart of these problems is your drinking. And so whether or not you agree, whether or not it's true, if you want to win your wife back, the alcohol needs to go.

You're trying to rebuild the trust and intimacy and respect between you and your wife.

What better way to start than by trusting and respecting her need for you to stop drinking.

The un-examined life is not worth living.

- Socrate

SUGGESTION #13
seek professional counseling

No, that's not a typo.

I had that printed teeny tiny small on purpose.

Because I know…

I know if there's anything an alcoholic (or any man for that matter) dreads more than *apologizing,* it's counseling. Most men would rather cut off their right one than go sit in a therapist's office and talk about their….*feelings!*

So I guess if you apologized in lieu of cutting off your left one (see suggestion #2), you still got two good nuts so you could take one for the team here. But if you didn't apologized – i.e. the left one's gone - or you just really, really (really!) don't like the idea of cutting off one of your balls, you might consider seeing a counselor.

I know it's all iky and womanly and not what you want to do but it can really help.

A lot.

And go by yourself!

That's right.

Don't go as a couple.

Go as an individual where you can let it all out…

But then don't have to see It all in your wife's eye.

Alcoholism is a disorder of both physiological and behavioral origin.

In other words, you are both chemically and psychologically driven to drink yourself into a shit-faced stupor over and over again.

And counseling isn't just about understanding the psychological component of addiction. A good, knowledgeable therapist can help you understand the chemical or physiological factors as well.

Go on, try it.

You've come this far.

What could it hurt?

And it just might help you…

Win your wife back!

A woman should soften but not weaken a man.

- Sigmund Freud

THE WIVES' SUGGESTIONS

Ok guys you are done!

Finito!

Off the hook!

I am truly humbled and honored that you stuck with me this far! (You are still there, right?) I hope at least some of what I have offered resonates with you and helps you in your efforts to save your marriage. But as I promised, it's not to be all-you-all-the-time. Your wife does have her own responsibilities to you, the marriage and even to your efforts to win her back. So these are my suggestions for you ladies.

First up, no drinking.

That's right.

No alcohol in the house, no ordering a glass of wine when you and your husband are out to dinner, no beer at the ballgame or July 4th picnic.

And you have to make it look effortless!

When he says, "don't you want a glass of wine" because you *always* order wine when you two go out to dinner, you have to be flawless in your denial.

"Nay, I don't care for one."

He may know or suspect you're doing it for him but you still have to make it look effortless. You can't be a martyr about it. If he asks, then sure you can acknowledge it's "for" him but you have to do it with a shrug and an air of "it's no big deal."

Your husband is an *addict!*

His brain is SCREAMING at him to drink!

His body is DEMANDING alcohol!

I know you're not the addict. I know you're not the one that needs to follow one beer, vodka tonic or shot of whiskey with 27 more. But your husband does. And no compassionate person could (should) argue that it's reasonable or kind to sit down next to an addict and sip on the very poison of his ills.

Second, you have to forgive him.

Hopefully he has apologized to you sincerely, with no qualifiers or caveats. And hopefully you have accepted it. Sincerely. With no caveats. And when you accepted that apology, it means you,

Have.

Accepted.

It.

The past is over.

It was ugly. God, it was ugly.

And painful. Very painful. And much of the pain is still there, inside you. What your brain doesn't remember consciously, your soul still probably carries subconsciously.

But...

If you want to stay...

And you've accepted his apology...

Then you have to put all that behind you and him.

I'm not saying you have to, or it's even possible, to forget the years of your husband's compulsive drinking and accompanying behavior.

Who could?

Alcoholism turns nice, good, loving, kind men into ass-holes!

And there are probably a few past events that were so painful as to haunt you still. By all means talk to him about these specifically. But you can't ask or expect him to apologize for every single individual infraction . I'm not letting him off the hook. I'm freeing you both so you can both move forward.

You're going to have to work to forgive him.

It's not going to come easy or naturally. (Who can easily forgive her husband for such things as regularly telling her to shut the fuck up or calling her a fucking bitch? What woman is going to "naturally" forgive the ruined holidays, the destroyed vacations and lost days?) No, you're not forgetting and it won't be easy to forgive but if you're going to stay, if you're going to accept his apology and his efforts to win you back, then you have to do your own work to forgive him.

Third, he doesn't owe you.

"WHAT?!" You scream.

"Oh yes he does (fucking!) OWE ME! Do you have ANY idea what he put me through?!"

Well now of course I know *exactly* what he put you through. Remember, I got my own AH. (Alcoholic husband. Or Ass Hole. Funny how that works out.) But if your husband is sincere in wanting to win you back and earnest in his efforts to win you back, you can't walk around like a queen expecting her husband-subject to fall at her feet.

Don't think for one minute your husband isn't ashamed, embarrassed, mortified, humiliated, broken, crushed, humbled – you get the idea – at his behavior. No alcoholic feels good about how he treated those around them, especially his wife. He feels diminished enough within himself without you walking around with his balls in your hand.

So if you're reading this book – and especially if you gave this book to your husband – and you're hanging around for him to try to win you back, you don't get to walk around like said queen and/or a martyr. After all, if he doesn't get to keep score for all the things he's doing in an effort to win you back, you don't get to keep a running tally of all he has to make up for.

Next up, stop complaining about your husband.

Hey, you don't need to tell me that when you are married to an alcoholic, there is *A LOT* to complain about! And I'll be the first one to say complaining has its cathartic place in this thing we call the human condition.

But…

There reaches a point (and it was probably several years back for all of us if we're honest with ourselves) where complaining is no longer a release but a trap. As in it traps within us all the negative emotions and feelings surrounding our husband's drinking, his behavior and the state of our marriage. When I became aware of the degree and depth of my complaining, I realized it was far more destructive than it was healing.

I kept my husband's alcoholism a secret for a very long time. That's a heavy, heavy burden to carry. I totally support and encourage you to find at least one person to whom you can confide in and share the pain and heartache of living with an alcoholic husband. When I finally confided in a true, trusted friend, my soul felt liberated. It was beneficial for me to lament and complain about my husband's behavior and/or our marriage and/or the dozens of beer cans littering my counter on a regular basis. Talking about, complaining about, even whining about things that are too hard to make sense of all by yourself is OK. It's justified. It's necessary. Human beings need to purge their souls. Mentally, Spiritually. Emotionally.It allows us to heal. Somewhat.

But there's a limit to the good of complaining.

There is a point where the complaining ceases to be a necessary part of mental health and survival and instead becomes *a nasty little indulgence and habit!*

It's like having an annoying, itchy bug bite on your arm that you just *have* to scratch.

Of course you have to scratch and claw and dig at the damn thing: all that vile bug-saliva coursing through your veins with its lousy anti-coagulating properties.

But if you kept clawing at it, it would start to hurt.

And then you'd break the skin.

And then it would start to bleed.

If you still continued, you would literally hit muscle. And then you'd hit tendons, ligaments and other soft, fleshy bits. Eventually you'd be clawing at *your bone!*

Whatever the original, legitimate and even justifiable need to scratch would have been satisfied long ago.

And you'd be digging and clawing out of some neurotic habit.

Complaining about your alcoholic husband is kind of like that.

Eventually it's neither cathartic nor cleansing.

It's just destructive and ruinous.

Let's be honest here:

There is nothing – nothing, nothing, nothing, NOTHING new for you to complain about anyway. It's all the same.

He's drinking.

He's drunk.

He's selfish.

He's checked out.

He's an asshole.

He's obnoxious.

After awhile even though the particulars may sound different – the complaining is all the same.

And it really is *very toxic.*

For you.

For your husband.

For your marriage.

Hey, I complained about my alcoholic husband with the best of them but eventually I knew I had to stop.

And he's not even reading a book on how to win me back!

You have to stop.

Regardless.

For your own mental health.

And if your husband is reading this book and making the effort to change…

You really, really, REALLY have to stop!

There is no way he will make any headway in his effort to regain your love and trust if you are keeping old hurts and transgressions alive through complaining about him. Even if he's not there to hear it. He'll know. Your soul will know.

So no more complaining.

(Not even about the toilet paper that he seems genetically incapable of putting on the roll!)

And finally…

Eventually…

If you've agreed to allow him to try to win you back…

You have to start *giving back.*

I know, I know.

You'd rather chew nails.

You are *so mad!!!!*

At him!

SO!!!!

MAD!!!

And it's an anger that runs deep. An anger of layers. An anger that started a long, long, LONG time ago and has been building – like a tiny snow ball rolling down a snow packed mountain side – ever since.

Of course you're mad!

You'd hardly be normal if you WEREN'T mad!!

And I know your first thought is something like,

"I don't care if he spends the next ten years doing every single thing in this book! I gave and I gave and I GAVE FOR YEARS without getting anything in return! Let him give and give for a few zillion years and see how it feels!"

I know!

I get it!

I DO!

My husband goes to work, comes home, watches TV and eats dinner before going to bed so he can get up and do the exact same thing the next day. And the next. And the next. And the next.

My husband does practically nothing around the house and he does even less for me or our the marriage!

If some chick told me that now because my husband has made some of the most basic and simplest efforts at change, I should start *giving back...*

I'd be like all WTF and such!

Hey, there is nothing fair or equitable, rational or sane about living with an alcoholic husband. It's pretty screwed up when he's drinking and it's pretty screwed up if and when he stops drinking and is trying to work his way back to you and sobriety.

You have to shoulder A LOT! And if you don't want to, that's OK.

If you're done, you're done.

No one can blame you!

But you have to be honest about what you want from your marriage and from your husband and what you are willing to give in return.

We can't all leave our alcoholic husbands – whether for financial reasons, religious or spiritual reasons, because of our children or just because we have a horse outback and couldn't take it to an apartment in the city.

If the marriage is over emotionally, then you should say the marriage is over emotionally. If you have to continue to live under the same roof for whatever reason, then find a way to live as reasonably good roommates.

But...

If you're going to let him try to repair the marriage...

If you want the marriage to be saved...

Then you have to pony up to the non-alcoholic bar yourself.

You may be surprised to find out how rewarding and rejuvenating it can be to be back in a marriage where your husband is present and working hard on participating once again.

We all know that women tend to give more than men do in relationships anyway. That's not a dig on men. It's just the nature of most women's beings. We like giving to our loved ones. It's actually one of the very real losses in the alcoholic marriage: we don't have that partner to whom we want to give of ourselves mentally, emotionally, spiritually and physically. I'm not saying you have to jump back in both feet all at once. Tip toe up to the shoreline. Put a toe or two in the water of giving. I used to make sure my husband had a clean towel in the bathroom every morning. If he decided to check back into the marriage, maybe I would try to do that for him again. You don't have to go all crazy-like-when-you-were-first-in-love giving. Just do little things. And as he works toward gaining your trust once again, you can work toward allowing yourself to be open and giving to him once again.

The best thing to hold onto in life is each other.

- Audrey Hepburn

THE END

So that's pretty much it guys (and dolls).

Some over-simplified advice for a situation that's anything but simple. If you've read this far, I am truly thankful and humbled.

Alcoholism is a nasty beast with the blood of your and your wife's soul dripping from its filthy claws. It feeds on everything that is your life – your marriage, your parenting, your self esteem, your hobbies, your interests. Your overall love and enthusiasm for life. It is giant and huge and menacing but also small and subtle and insidious.

And it has fed on your wife's life and soul as well.

It has made her cry more than you will ever know.

It has made her hate you and love you and hate still loving you.

It's made her curse you name.

And shake in fear for what you are doing to yourself.

It's had her walking out the door, leaving you, divorcing you…running you over with the car. Ok, maybe not that one. Well, maybe. In her mind anyway.

The point is your compulsive drinking has evoked *Every. Emotion. Imaginable* within your wife. No one gets away from the beast of alcoholism unscathed. Her injuries aren't the same as yours but they are just as grave.

The number one thing the Beast hates is honesty. Like kryptonite to Superman, honesty makes the Beast shrivel up and die. And so that is my final suggestion to you.

Be honest.
Be honest if you drink again.
Be honest if you're afraid of drinking again.
Be honest about what you can give her.
Be honest about what you can't.
And be honest with yourself.
No one likes drinking compulsively.
Not even the alcoholic.
Recovery isn't easy but right now, you have a woman who loves you, who wants to still love you, who is trying to hold onto loving you.

There is only one happiness in life, to love and be loved.

- George Sand

ABOUT THE AUTHOR

Wren Waters is a writer, mother and the wife of an alcoholic. When she was first coming to terms with being married to an alcoholic, she found the information and resources available to her limited. And what little information there was seemed to follow the same "party line:" She was co-dependent. She was an enabler. She should hate the drinking but love the man.

With her first book, "The Alcoholic Husband Primer: Survival Skills For The Alcoholic's Wife" Waters hoped to offer women the advice she felt she would have benefited from in the early years of her marriage as she learned to live with an alcoholic husband.

With this book, "So You Want To Win Her Back…" she hopes she can give the alcoholic husband some "insider's tips" on what it's really like to be married to him and what it is his wife needs in order to stay in the marriage.

CONTACT:

WrenRWaters@gmail.com

Made in the USA
Las Vegas, NV
05 January 2023

65030911R00046